Clean Jokes For Senior

INTRODUCTION

WE HOPE THESE JOKES BRIGHTEN YOUR DAYS, SPARK NOSTALGIA, AND MAYBE EVEN INSPIRE A FEW LAUGHS TO SHARE WITH FRIENDS AND LOVED ONES.

YOUR FEEDBACK IS INVALUABLE TO US, SO PLEASE CONSIDER LEAVING A REVIEW AND SHARING YOUR FAVORITE JOKES WITH OTHERS.

1. Why don't scientists trust atoms?

Because they make up everything!

---

2. What did one wall say to the other wall?

I'll meet you at the corner!

3. Why don't we ever tell secrets on a farm?

Because the potatoes have eyes, the corn has ears, and the beans stalk.

4. Why did the scarecrow win an award?

Because he was outstanding in his field!

---

5. What's orange and sounds like a parrot?

A carrot!

6. What do you call a fake noodle?

An Impasta!

7. How does a penguin build its house?

Igloos it together!

---

8. What do you call a bear with no teeth?

A gummy bear!

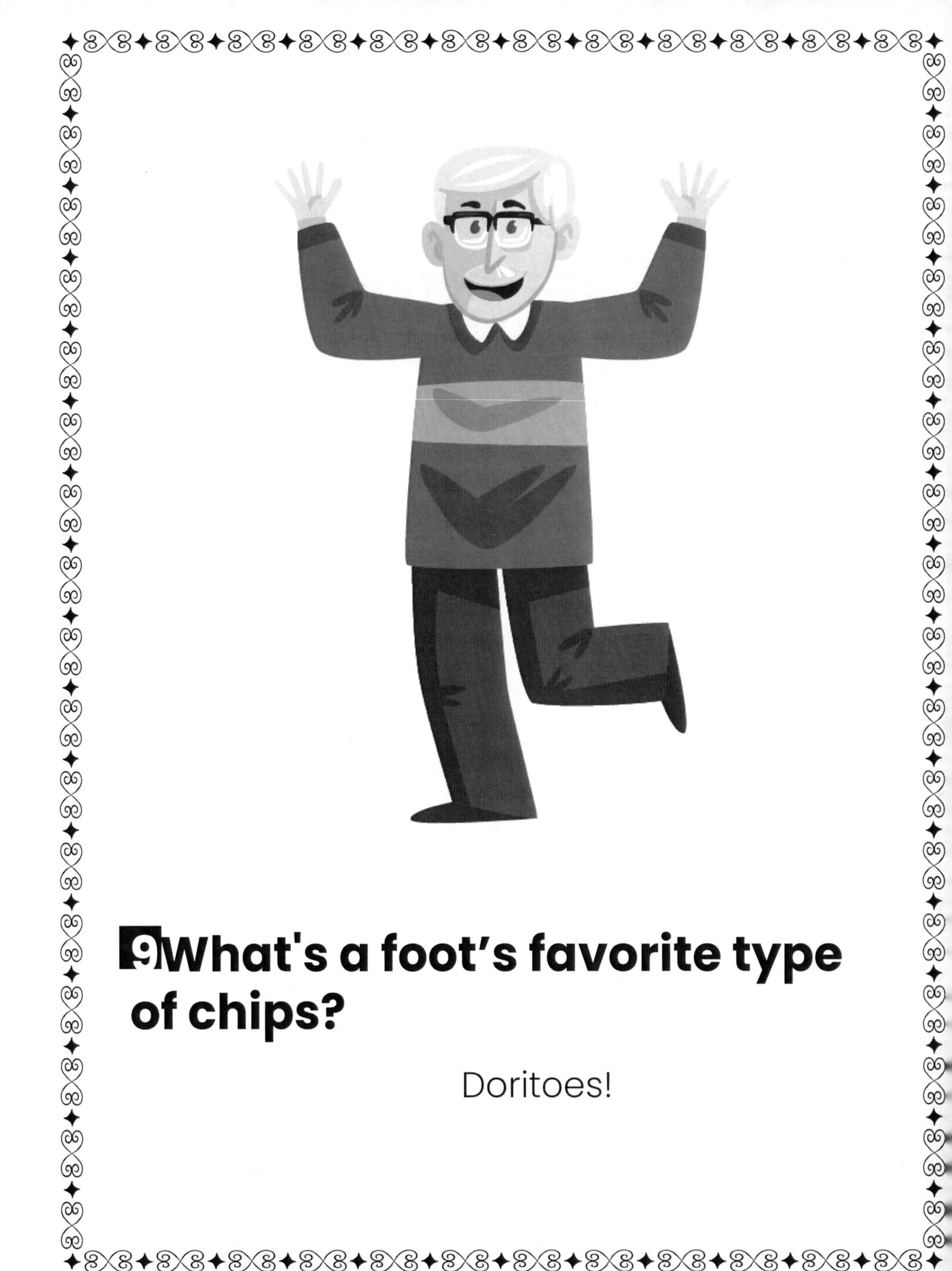

9. What's a foot's favorite type of chips?

Doritoes!

10 How does a cucumber become a pickle?

It goes through a jarring experience!

---

11 Why did the math book look sad?

Because it had too many problems!

12 **How do you organize a space party?**

You planet!

13 What do you call cheese that isn't yours?

Nacho cheese!

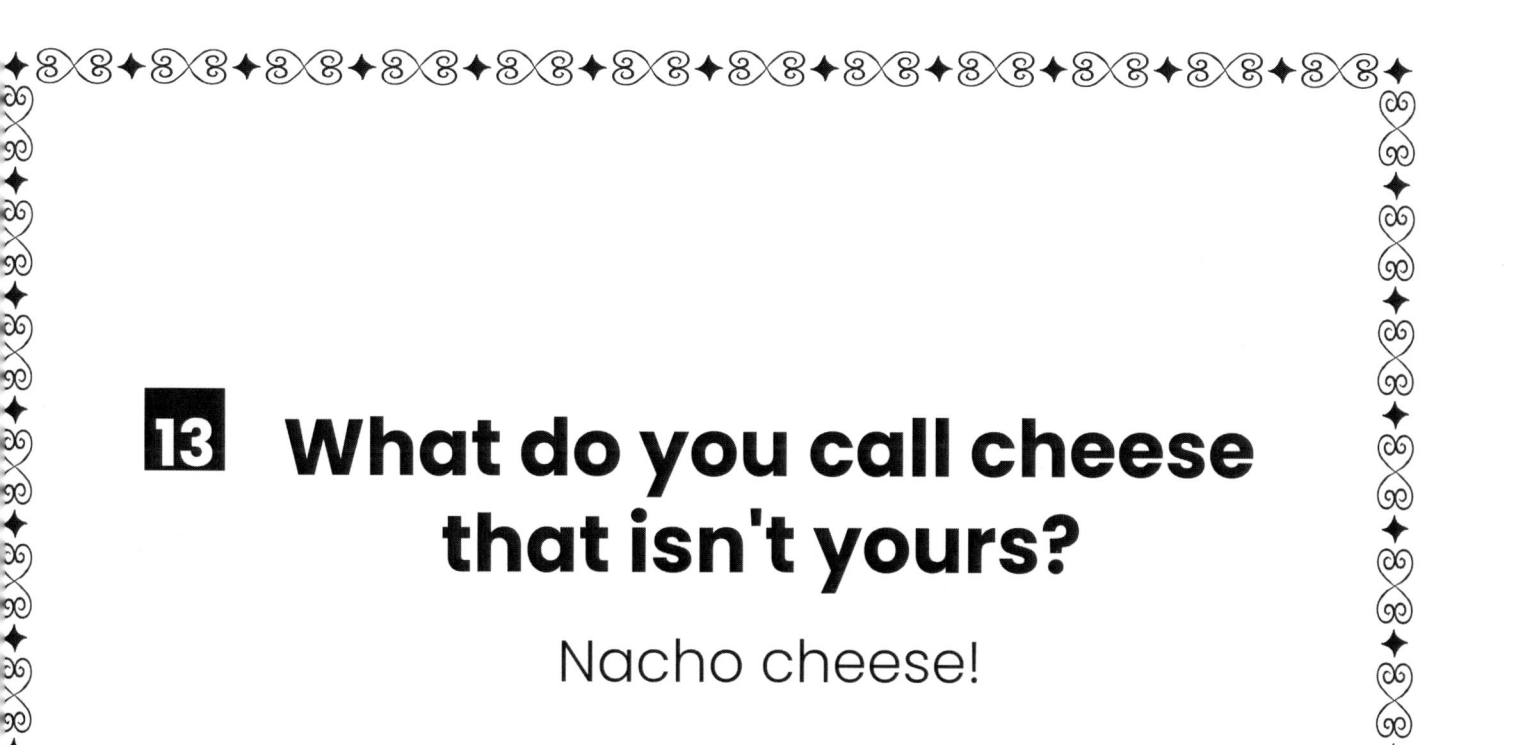

14 What does a cloud wear under his raincoat?

Thunderwear!

15 What kind of shoes do spies wear?

Sneakers!

16 **Why was the belt arrested?**

It was holding up a pair of pants!

---

17 **Why did the bicycle fall over?**

It was two tired!

18. What do you call a snowman with a suntan?

A puddle!

19 **What kind of music do mummies listen to?**

Wrap music!

---

20 **Why couldn't the leopard play hide and seek?**

Because he was always spotted!

21 What kind of tree fits in your hand?

A palm tree!

22 How do you catch a squirrel?

Climb a tree and act like a nut!

---

23 What do you call a snowman that tells tall tales?

A snow-fake!

24 What did the big flower say to the little flower?

Hi, bud!

25 Why was the broom late?

It over swept!

---

26 What does a nosy pepper do?

Gets jalapeno business!

27 What do you call a fish without eyes?

Fish!

28 **What do you call a boomerang that won't come back?**

A stick!

---

29 **What do you call a man with a rubber toe?**

Roberto!

30 **Why did the golfer change his pants?**

Because he got a hole in one!

31 How does a train eat?

It goes chew chew!

---

32 Why don't skeletons fight each other?

They don't have the guts!

33 How do you make holy water?

You boil the hell out of it!

34 **Why don't oysters donate to charity?**

Because they are shellfish!

---

35 **Why don't some fish play piano?**

They're scared they'll hit the wrong key and end up in a different scale!

36 How do you make a tissue dance?

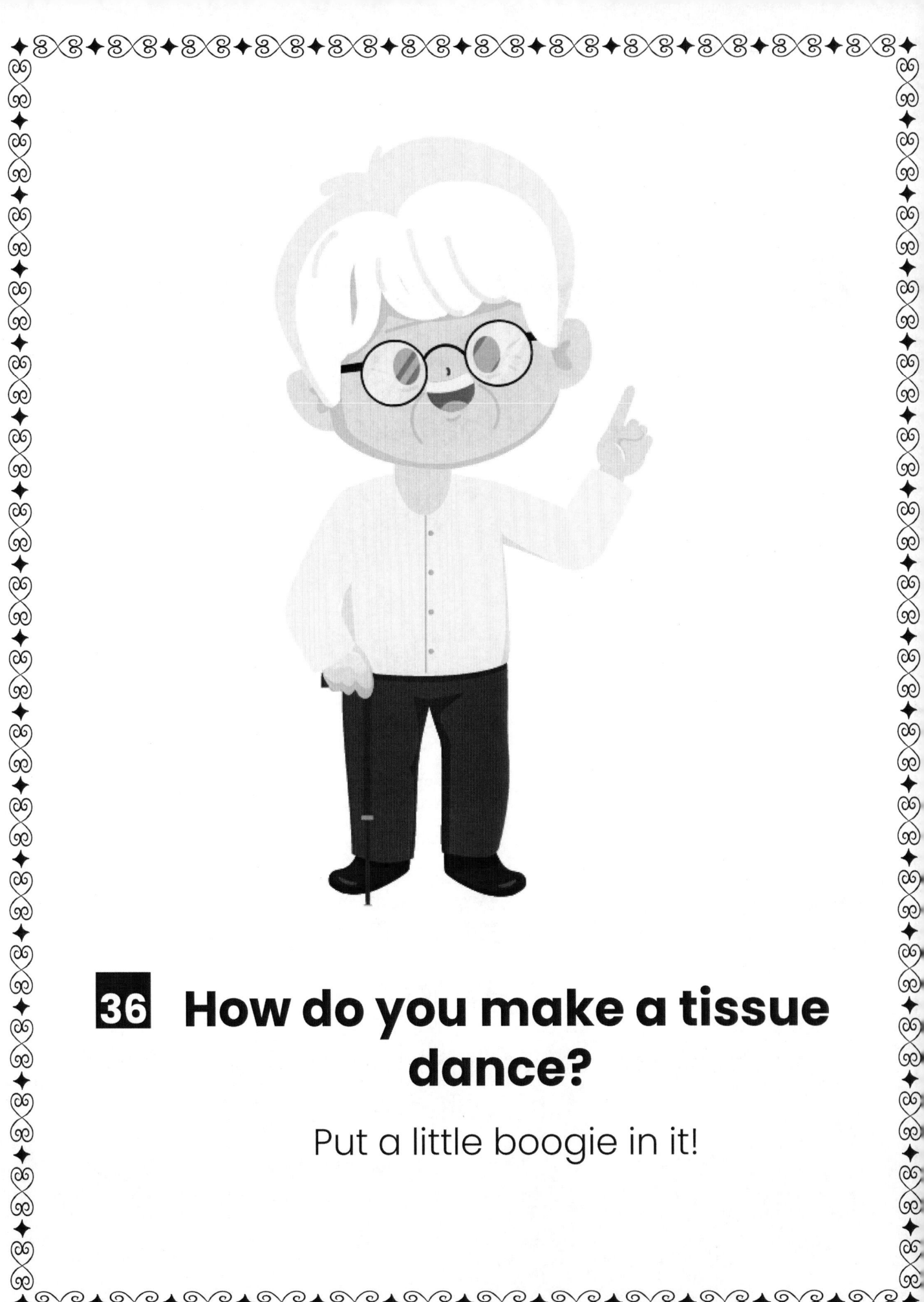

Put a little boogie in it!

37. Why did the cookie go to the doctor?

Because it felt crummy!

---

38. Why did the stadium get hot after the game?

All of the fans left!

39 **What did the traffic light say to the car?**

Don't look, I'm about to change!

40 **Why can't you trust a map?**

Because they always point out your flaws!

---

41 **What do you call a can opener that doesn't work?**

A can't opener!

42 **What do you call a deer with no eyes?**

No idea!

43 How do trees access the internet?

They log in!

---

44 What's a light bulb's favorite kind of joke?

A bright one!

45 Why don't ants get sick?

Because they have anty-bodies!

46 **Why did the can crusher quit his job?**

Because it was soda pressing!

---

47 **Why did the picture go to jail?**

Because it was framed!

48 How do you stop a bull from charging?

Take away its credit card!

49 **Why did the melon jump into the lake?**

It wanted to be a watermelon!

_____

50 **What do you call a group of musical whales?**

An Orca-stra!

51 What do you call a bear with no socks on?

Bare-foot!

52 **Why did the teddy bear say no to dessert?**

Because he was already stuffed!

---

53 **What kind of key opens a banana?**

A monkey!

54 **What did the zero say to the eight?**

Nice belt!

55 **Why don't eggs tell each other jokes?**

Because they can crack each other up!

_____

56 **What's a construction worker's favorite type of math?**

Geometry, because it's all about the angles!

57 Why don't basketball players get sunburned?

Because they always stay in the shade!

58 **How do we know that the ocean is friendly?**

It always waves!

---

59 **What do you call a sheep with no legs?**

A cloud!

60 What is a cat's favorite color?

Purrr-ple!

61 **How do you make a milkshake?**

Give a cow a pogo stick!

---

62 **Why don't aliens eat clowns?**

Because they taste funny!

63 What kind of music scares balloons?

Pop music!

64 How does a mouse feel after a shower?

Squeaky clean!

---

65 Why don't tennis players get married?

Because love means nothing to them!

66 Why did the jelly wobble?

Because it saw the milk shake!

67 **What's a ghost's favorite dessert?**

I scream!

---

68 **What did the fish say when it hit the wall?**

Dam!

69 **What's a tree's favorite drink?**

Root beer!

70 **Why did the girl bring a ladder to the bar?**

Because she heard the drinks were on the house!

---

71 **Why can't you play hide and seek with mountains?**

Because they always peak!

72 Why did the banana go to the party?

Because it was a-peeling!

73 **Why don't they allow loud laughing in Hawaii?**

Because it's a low "ha" state!

---

74 **What do you get when you cross a snake and a pie?**

A pie-thon!

75 **What do you call a dinosaur with an extensive vocabulary?**

A thesaurus!

76 **What do you get when you cross a snowman and a vampire?**

Frostbite!

---

77 **How do you catch a whole school of fish?**

With bookworms!

78 **What's an astronaut's favorite place on a computer?**

The space bar!

79 **What do you call a cat who swallowed a duck?**

A duck-filled-fatty-pus!

---

80 **How does a dog stop a video?**

By hitting the paws button!

81. What's the best way to carve wood?

Whittle by whittle!

82 **What's an artist's favorite type of clothing?**

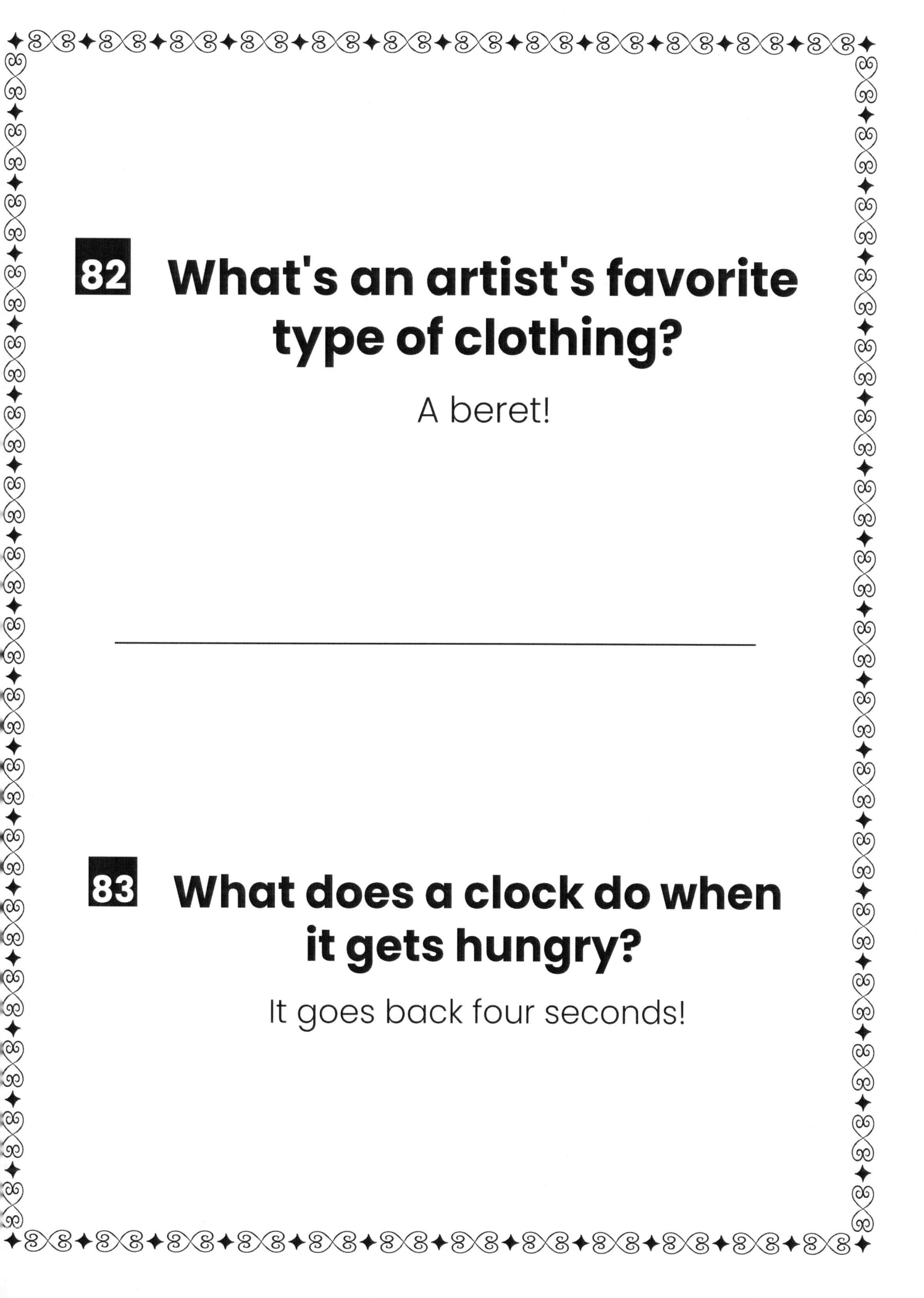

A beret!

---

83 **What does a clock do when it gets hungry?**

It goes back four seconds!

84 **What did one hat say to the other hat?**

You stay here, I'll go on ahead!

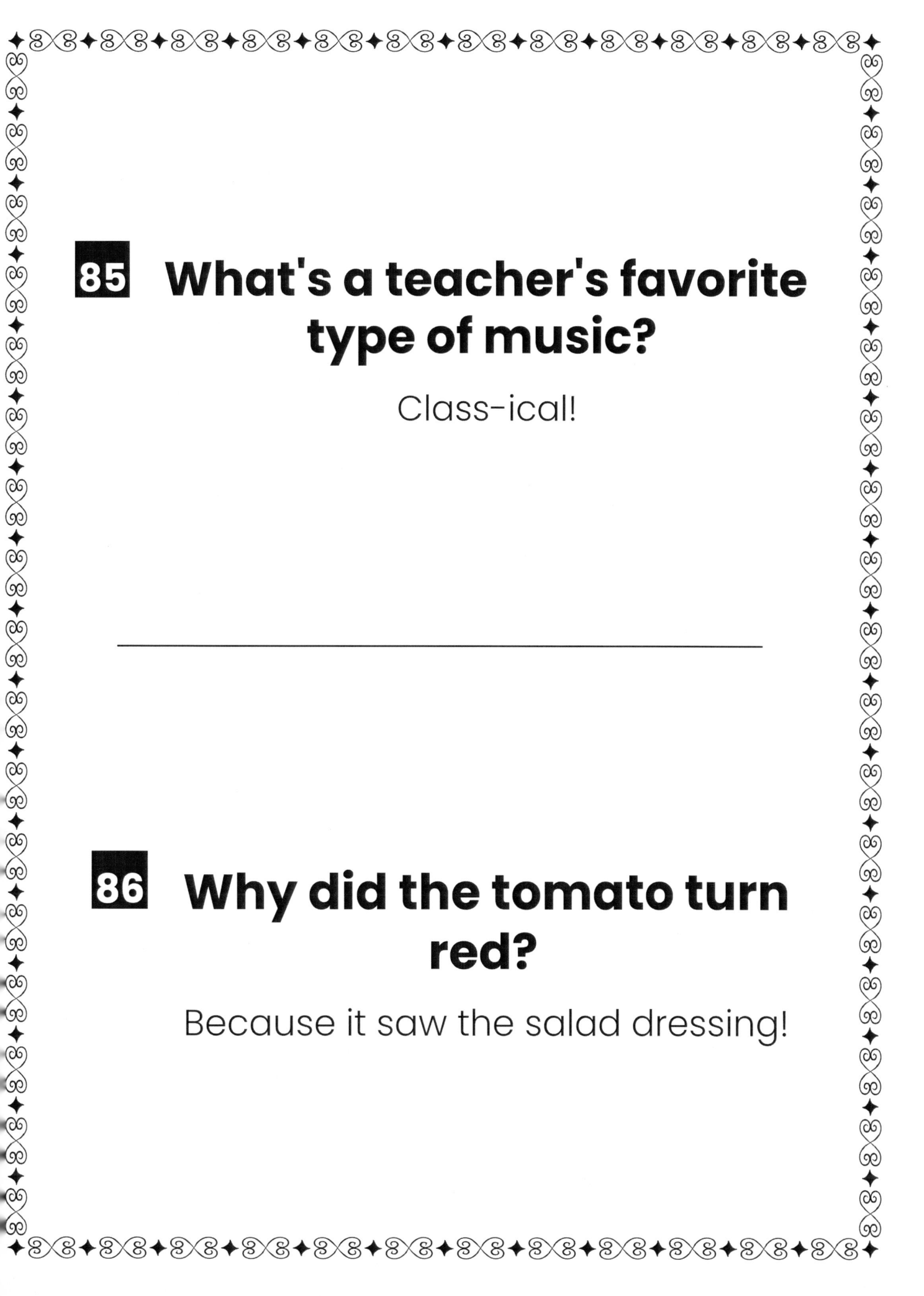

85 **What's a teacher's favorite type of music?**

Class-ical!

---

86 **Why did the tomato turn red?**

Because it saw the salad dressing!

87 Why did the man put his money in the blender?

Because he wanted to make some liquid assets!

88 What do you call a parade of rabbits hopping backwards?

A receding hare-line!

89 How do you know if an ant is a boy or a girl?

They're all girls, otherwise they'd be uncles.

90 **Why did the boy sprinkle sugar on his pillow?**

He wanted to have sweet dreams!

91 **How does a scientist freshen her breath?**

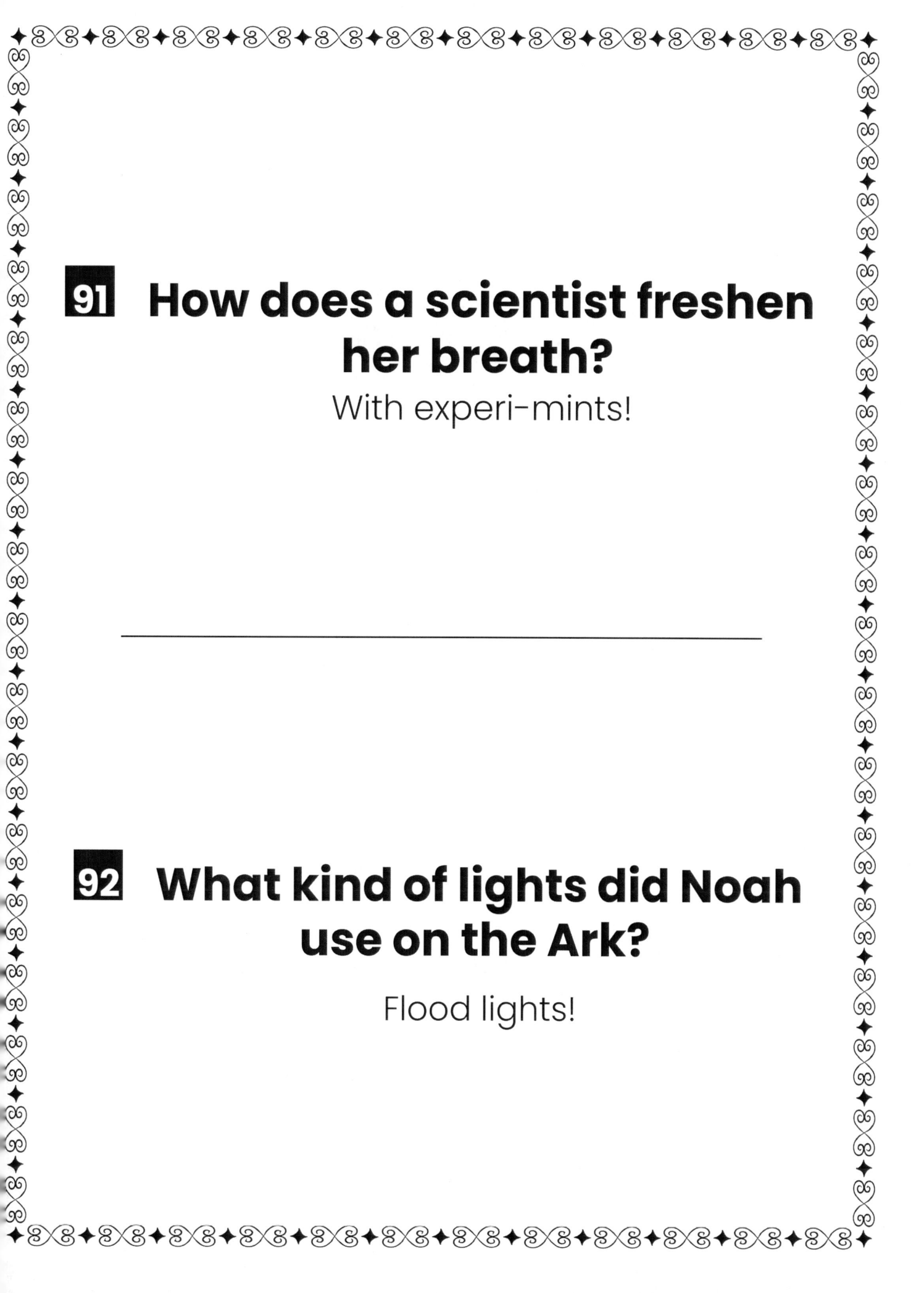

With experi-mints!

---

92 **What kind of lights did Noah use on the Ark?**

Flood lights!

93 **What did the ocean say to the sailboat?**

Nothing, it just waved!

94 **Why can't you give Elsa a balloon?**

Because she will let it go!

---

95 **Why couldn't the bicycle find its way home?**

It lost its bearings!

96 **How do you turn soup into gold?**

Add 24 carrots!

97 Why did the coffee file a police report?

It got mugged!

---

98 Why did the gardener plant light bulbs?

He wanted to grow a power plant!

99 **What do you call a snake who works for the government?**

A civil serpent!

100 **What's a tailor's favorite kind of salad?**

Seamstress dressing!

---

101 **What's an astronaut's favorite board game?**

Moon-opoly!

102 **What did the grape say when it got stepped on?**

Nothing, but it let out a little wine!

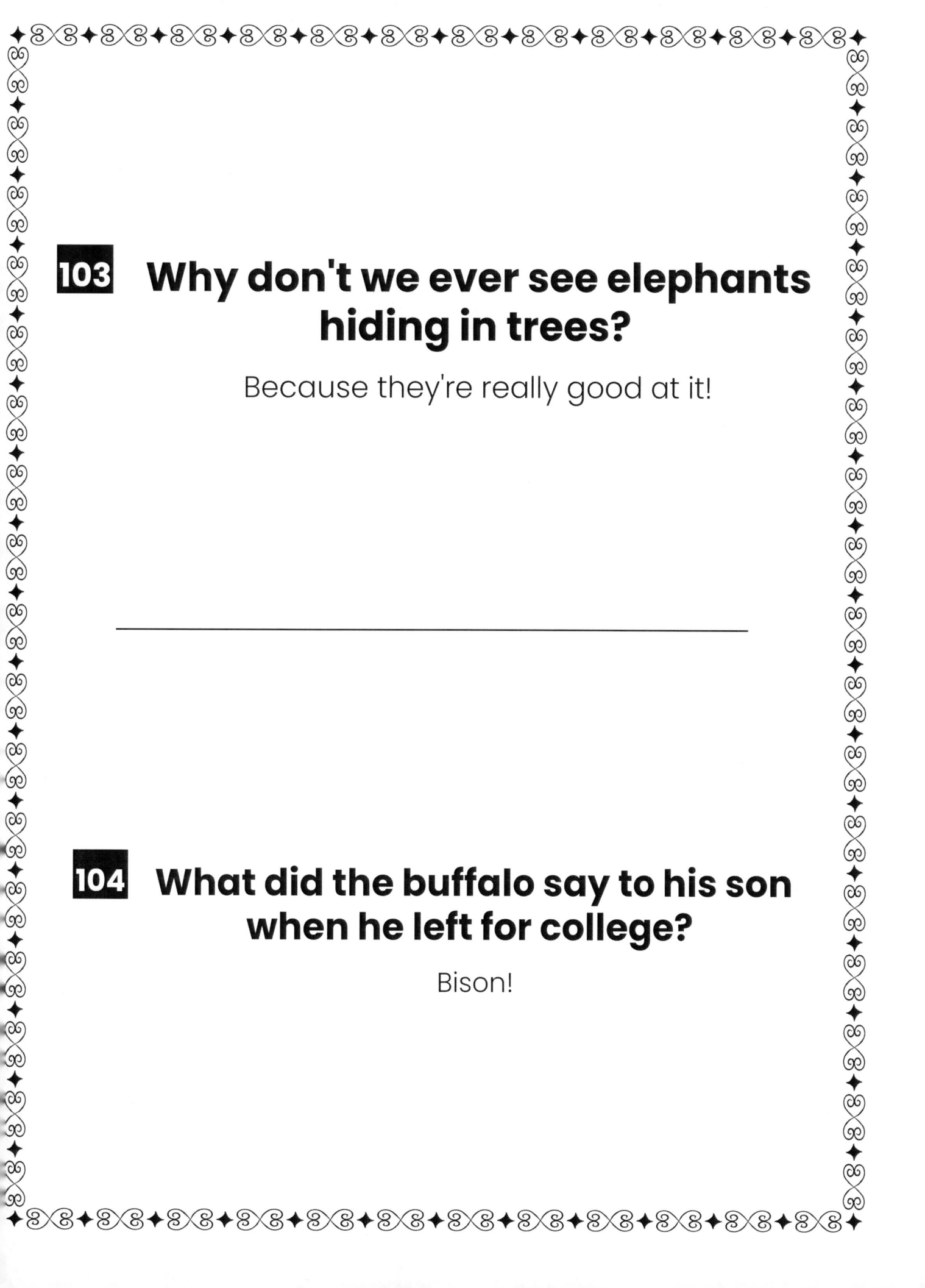

103 **Why don't we ever see elephants hiding in trees?**

Because they're really good at it!

---

104 **What did the buffalo say to his son when he left for college?**

Bison!

105 **Why did the school kids eat their homework?**

Because the teacher told them it was a piece of cake!

106 What kind of award did the inventor of knock knock jokes win?

The "no-bell" prize!

---

107 Why don't we tell secrets in a cornfield?

Because there are too many ears!

108 What does a cloud with an itchy rash do?

Find the nearest "sky-n" doctor!

109 Why did the music note go to school?

It wanted to improve its "composure"!

110 Why did the computer go to the doctor?

It had a "virus"!

111. What's the hardest part about writing a book?

Creating a "novel" idea!

112 Why did the math teacher visit the beach?

She was on a quest for the "root" of all tides!

---

113 Why was the math problem so easy?

It was a "piece of pi"!

114 Why did the sun go to school?

To get a little "brighter"!

115 **Why did the kid study in the airplane?**

He wanted a higher education!

---

116 **Why did the kid bring a ladder to school?**

Because he wanted to go to high school!

117 **What do you call a story told by a giraffe?**

A tall tale!

118. Why did the computer take its glasses?

It lost its "windows"!

---

119. Why do we tell actors to break a leg?

Because every play has a cast!

120 **What do you call a funny mountain?**

Hill-arious!

121 **Why was the computer cold?**
It left its "windows" open!

---

122 **What do you call a magic dog?**
A Labracadabrador!

123 **Why did the smartphone go to school?**

It wanted to have more "class"!

"Laughter is the best medicine, especially for seniors.
It's a great way to relieve stress, improve mood, and boost health."

LOOK AT THE OTHER PARTS OF OUR JOKES!